Helping Children See Jesus

ISBN: 978-1-64104-002-0

Joseph Part 1
Old Testament Volume 4:
Genesis Part 4

Author: Arlene Piepgrass
Illustrator: Vernon Henkel
Computer Graphic Artist: Andrew Cross
Typesetting and Layout: Morgan Melton, Patricia Pope

© 2018 Bible Visuals International
PO Box 153, Akron, PA 17501-0153
Phone: (717) 859-1131
www.biblevisuals.org

All rights reserved. No part of this publication may be reproduced, stored in a retrieval system or transmitted in any form by any means, electronic, mechanical, photocopy, recording or otherwise, without the prior permission of the publisher, except as provided by USA copyright law.

RELATED ITEMS

To access related items (such as activities, memory verse posters and translated texts) please visit our web store at shop.biblevisuals.org and enter 2004 in the search box on the page.

FREE TEXT DOWNLOAD

To access a FREE printable copy of the teaching text (PDF format) in English or other available languages, enter S2004DL in the search box. Add the item to your cart, and use coupon code XTACSV17 at checkout. Once your order is processed you will receive an email with a link to the free download.

"God was with him, And delivered him out of all his afflictions . . ."

Acts 7:9b-10a

Lesson 1
RELATIONSHIP WITH THE FATHER (Part 1)

NOTE TO THE TEACHER

The events of the Old Testament occurred hundreds of years before those in the New Testament. Yet there are various accounts recorded in the Old Testament which picture (or illustrate) New Testament truths. Some Bible facts may be hard for us to understand. So God, the Author of the Bible, often helps us by using things we do understand to picture those that are difficult. Some of these word-pictures are called "types." A type can be an object, a person, a custom or a happening. It is real itself. But it pictures something far greater than itself.

Joseph is not referred to in the New Testament as a *type* of Christ. But many of his experiences were *like* the experiences Christ had in His life. God seems to have given us beforehand (in Joseph) a picture showing what His Son would be like 1,900 years later. Thus the title for this volume and the next: *Joseph, a Picture of the Lord Jesus.*

As you will see, in this first series we have two illustrations from the life of Joseph, followed by two from the life of Christ. Depending upon the age and ability of your students, you may prefer to make two lessons out of one. If so, you will use alternate illustrations. (In lesson #1, for example, illustrations #1 and #3 for the first lesson.)

Please explain that all conversation in the lessons is not exact, but as it *may* have been.

Scripture to be studied: Genesis 37; all verses mentioned in the lesson

The *aim* of the lesson: To lead my students to a deeper understanding of the Lord Jesus Christ through the Old Testament picture of Joseph.

What your students should *know*: While Joseph may be *like* the Lord Jesus in certain ways, Christ is greater, more wonderful.

What your students should *feel*: Amazement that God would reveal through Joseph, hundreds of years beforehand, something of what His own dear Son would be like.

What your students should *do*:
  Unsaved: Place their trust in the Saviour who died for their sins.
  Saved: Determine to study the Bible more carefully so they will see other likenesses between Joseph and the Lord Christ.

Lesson outline (for the teacher's and students' notebooks):
1. Joseph, the beloved son (Genesis 37:3-4).
2. Joseph and his father (Genesis 37:10-13; compare Genesis 49:22-26; 50:1-14).
3. Jesus, the beloved Son (Matthew 3:17; 17:5).
4. Jesus and God His Father (John 1:1-3; 1 Peter 1:18-20).

The verse to be memorized:

God was with him, And delivered him out of all his afflictions. (Acts 7:9b-10a)

THE LESSON

Has anyone ever told you, "You are exactly like your father"? Or, "You look just like your mother"? (*Teacher:* Encourage students to discuss how they are like their parents.)

It is not at all unusual for people to be like those who lived *before* them. This has always been true–even in Bible times. But there is something surprisingly different recorded in the Bible. Some who lived in Old Testament times are like those who lived *afterward*–even hundreds of years after! The history of one such person is given in the very first Bible book, Genesis. Some of Joseph's experiences are much like those of Another. God seems to have given us in this Old Testament man a preview of One who appears in the New Testament. Listen carefully.

Jacob, whom we studied in the last series, was a trickster. In time, he reaped what he sowed. For seven years he had worked in Haran for his Uncle Laban. In return he was to receive Laban's younger daughter, Rachel. But instead of getting Rachel as his wife, Jacob got Leah, her older sister. His uncle had tricked him! Jacob was angry and brokenhearted.

"Don't be upset, Jacob," Laban said smoothly. "I'll also give you Rachel now if you will work seven more years for her–without wages!"

So Jacob had two wives instead of one. Because of his special love for Rachel, this meant trouble for Jacob right from the beginning of his family life.

1. JOSEPH, THE BELOVED SON
Genesis 37:3-4

As the years went by, Leah had several baby boys. Rachel had none. Altogether, ten sons were born to Jacob. Still Rachel had no children. She loved Jacob dearly. Often she prayed, "Dear God, please give Jacob and me a baby!"

God heard her prayers. (See Genesis 30:22.) And He gave them a baby boy whom they named Joseph. How happy they were!

Jacob loved all his sons. But he loved Joseph most because he was the son of his favorite wife. Later, Jacob took his family back to their homeland, Canaan. On the way, Joseph's brother, Benjamin, was born and their mother Rachel died. Now Jacob loved Rachel's sons even more.

Show Illustration #1

When Joseph was a teenager, his father made him a special coat. Giving the coat to Joseph, Jacob said, "My son, God has promised to bless our family and multiply it. One day you will be the leader of our tribe. Wear this coat. When others see it they will know I have a special love for you. They will understand that you have a place of honor."

From that day on there was no doubt about Jacob's love for Joseph. It was plain to everyone.

2. JOSEPH AND HIS FATHER
Genesis 37:10-13; 49:22-26; 50:1-14

The Bible does not tell us anything about Joseph's early life. But it does tell us what happened to his father, Jacob, during those years. While the older brothers were off tending the sheep, Jacob and Joseph talked often about many things.

"Joseph, do you remember when we lived in Haran? I worked there 20 years for Uncle Laban. God blessed me with many herds and servants. He gave me a fine family. But the day came when God told me to return to my own country (Genesis 31:3, 12). So we packed our things and started home."

Show Illustration #2

"Yes, Father, I remember. That was a long, hard trip. And I'll never forget the morning you limped into camp. Even though you couldn't walk properly, the look on your face told us something wonderful had happened."

"What a night that was!" Jacob recalled. "I had been stubborn. I always wanted my own way. But God didn't let me have my way. That night, while the rest of you slept, God wrestled with me. He touched my thigh and I have limped ever since. I saw God face-to-face that night. (See Genesis 32:30.) Since then my life has never been the same. I have been a changed man. Oh, I've made mistakes. But because of my lameness, I remember who is Master, and I have really learned to trust God."

"Remember our visit to Bethel, Father? You showed us the spot where you saw the ladder from earth to Heaven. I wish I could have seen, as you did, the angels going up and down that ladder." (See Genesis 35:1-7; 28:11-22.)

"Joseph, that first night in Bethel was amazing. There I realized what a sinner I was. I understood that God alone could save me. I did see angels there. But I also saw the Lord Himself. I heard His voice. 'Jacob,' God said, 'I will keep you wherever you go. I will not leave you.' And, Joseph, He has kept His word!" Jacob added firmly.

Quietly he continued, "God promised to give us this land and to multiply our family. Someday, Joseph, you will be the one to receive all God's Promises. You will rule over our family." (See Genesis 35:1-15.)

Jacob and Joseph shared many happy days together. Often they spoke of what God had done. They talked of what He would do, according to His promises. Joseph loved his father. And like his father, Joseph loved the true and living God.

From this little bit of Joseph's early life, we have learned two truths: (1) Joseph was loved by his father in a special way and (2) Joseph and his father enjoyed being together. Someone who lived much, much later was especially loved by His Father. He and His Father enjoyed being together. Think now! Of whom am I talking? (*Teacher:* Encourage class discussion.)

3. JESUS, THE BELOVED SON
Matthew 3:17; 17:5

The Lord Jesus Christ is the One who is like Joseph. Joseph was loved by his father, Jacob. The Lord Jesus was loved by His father, God. The coat young Joseph wore announced that his father had a special love for him. About 1,900 years later, the Lord Jesus came to earth.

Show Illustration #3

When He was a grown man, Jesus was baptized. As He was coming up out of the water, the heavens opened. God the Father announced, "This is My beloved Son, in whom I am well pleased" (Matthew 3:17).

Almost three years later, Jesus was on a mountaintop with three of His disciples. Again God spoke from Heaven saying, "This is My beloved Son, in whom I am well pleased; hear ye Him" (Matthew 17:5).

When the Lord Jesus was teaching His followers, He spoke many times of His Father's love for Him. (See, for example: John 5:20; 10:17; 15:9.) Jesus said God loved Him even before the world was created. (See John 17:24.)

4. JESUS AND GOD HIS FATHER
John 1:1-3; 1 Peter 1:18-20

We may not understand how God the Father and Christ the Son were together without a beginning. But it's true because God's Word says it. (See John 1:1-2; 17:5; Colossians 1:17.) We don't know all that happened before time began. The Bible does give certain facts, however.

Together, God the Father and Christ the Son planned and created everything. They made the heavens, the earth, the sky, the seas, trees, animals, birds, man and woman. (See Genesis 1:1-2:25; John 1:3; Colossians 1:16.) But they knew, even before creation, that Adam, the first man, would sin. They knew that everyone born after Adam would sin.

So even before the world was formed, God the Father and God the Son decided on a wonderful plan. The Lord Jesus Christ would leave Heaven and come into the world. By His life, He would show people how God wants them to live. They would see that they were not living His way, but sinfully. Because of this, the Lord Jesus would take the punishment for the sins of all the world. (See 1 Peter 1:18-20; 2:24; 1 John 4:14.) He would rise again from the dead so that all who put their complete trust in Him could be in right relationship with God. (See Romans 4:25; 2 Corinthians 5:21.)

The Father and Son planned for a special kind of family. And they want *you* to be in that family. Would you like to be in the family of God? If so, this is what you must do: believe that the Lord Jesus Christ is the Son of God (1 John 4:15); believe that He died and rose again for you, a sinner; place all your trust in Him. When you truly do this, you become one of God's children–a member of His family. (See John 1:12.)

Show Illustration #4

A family needs a place to live. So the Father and the Son are together now in Heaven, preparing a glorious home. One day each member of their family will live with them forever and ever. Heaven is more beautiful than we can imagine. There is no night there because the shining brightness of God and Christ light Heaven all the time. (See Revelation 21:23.) There is no sin there. (See Revelation 21:27.) This means there is no wickedness, sickness, sorrow or tears. These all result from sin. There will be beautiful dwelling places in Heaven (John 14:2-3). God and Christ have done all they can to make it possible for you to be with them there.

Long before you were born, long before your grandparents were born, long, long before Jacob and his son Joseph talked together, God the Father and Christ were together in beautiful Heaven. What joy they had there! But Jesus left it all and came to this wicked, sinful earth to take our sins upon Himself. (See Philippians 2:5-8; Isaiah 53:6; 1 Peter 2:24.) Why? Because He loves us and wants us for His own.

Have you placed all your trust in the Lord Jesus? If not, will you do so right now?

Between now and the time we next meet, study more about Joseph in the Bible. Try to find other likenesses between him and Christ in Genesis 37.

Lesson 2
RELATIONSHIP WITH THE FATHER (Part 2)

NOTE FOR THE TEACHER

The Bible is an amazing book! Hidden in the Old Testament are illustrations of New Testament truths. For example, many experiences which Joseph (of the Old Testament) had during his lifetime were like those of the Lord Jesus Christ (recorded in the New Testament). We would learn a great deal by studying about Joseph only. But we better understand the meaning of the events in his life when we compare them with those which Christ had. For the New Testament makes clear the hidden truths of the Old Testament.

If you are like the greatest of all Teachers, the Lord Jesus Christ, you use object lessons. On one occasion, for instance, He began, "A sower went out to sow his seed." He then told what happened when that seed (His object lesson) was sown in various kinds of soil. His hearers needed an explanation of the object lesson. So He taught, "The seed is the Word of God." (See Luke 8:5-11.) By itself the story was clear. But He used it to teach a far greater truth.

So it is with certain people, events and things in the Old Testament. They are clear. They teach wonderful truths. But when we study the New Testament, we understand more fully the meaning of the Old Testament truths. And, by taking our study seriously, these truths will affect the way we live. (For example, see 1 Corinthians 10:6.)

As you know, teacher, the Joseph of our lesson lived about 1,900 years before the Joseph in whose home the Lord Jesus was reared. Use the inside back cover to help your students remember that the two Josephs are not the same.

Scripture to be studied: Genesis 37; all verses mentioned in the lesson.

The *aim* of the lesson: To lead your students to a deeper appreciation of the relationship of God the Father and Christ the Son.

What your students should *know*: Joseph's obedience to his earthly father illustrates Christ's obedience to the heavenly Father.

What your students should *feel*: Overwhelmed that God the Son would give His all for us sinners.

What your students should *do*:
  Unsaved: Accept the salvation which Christ has purchased with His blood.
  Saved: Obey God's commands in their relationships with others.

Lesson outline (for the teacher's and students' notebooks):
1. Joseph, sent by his father (Genesis 37:13).
2. Joseph obeys his father (Genesis 37:13-17).
3. The Lord Jesus, sent by His Father (John 3:16; 1 John 4:10).
4. The Lord Jesus obeys His Father (Luke 19:10; John 4:34; 5:30).

The verse to be memorized:

God was with him, And delivered him out of all his afflictions. (Acts 7:9b-10a)

THE LESSON

Have you ever looked down at the earth on a sunny day and exclaimed, "There's a bird flying overhead!"? You didn't see it, for it was in back of you. Nor did you hear it. Yet you were certain a bird was there. How did you know? (*Teacher:* Encourage class discussion.) Because you saw the shadow of the bird, you knew the bird was above.

Just so, in the Old Testament there are certain people, things and events which are like shadows. God has purposely caused these shadows so we can know New Testament truths in advance. Have you read of Joseph in Genesis 37? Did you see likenesses, shadows of the Lord Jesus? (*Teacher:* Allow student participation.) Listen carefully. Try to find shadows of the Lord Jesus as we continue our study of Joseph.

Jacob, the father of Joseph, had a large family. He had 12 sons and one daughter. Why was Joseph especially dear to Jacob? (*Joseph was the first son of Jacob's favorite wife, Rachel. Jacob worked 14 years to get her. Rachel later died when Joseph's little brother, Benjamin, was born.*) Joseph loved God. He wanted to follow God's plan for his life. This gave Jacob a special love for Joseph.

But Jacob loved all his sons. He was concerned for them. The ten oldest were shepherds. Daily they took their large flocks to find water and grass. Day after day they roamed farther from home. Jacob and his two youngest sons stayed close to their tents in Hebron.

At night the shepherds were too far away to return to the camp of their father. They simply slept out under the stars. Weeks went by. The flocks ate all the grass. So the shepherds led them farther away from Jacob's tent.

1. JOSEPH, SENT BY HIS FATHER
Genesis 37:13

Finally, when they were gone a long time, Jacob became concerned. He decided something had to be done. There was no postal or telephone service in those days. So he couldn't receive letters or calls from his sons. The only way to get news was to send a messenger to them. So he called Joseph, saying, "Your brothers have gone to Shechem to find pasture for their flocks. (Shechem was about 50 miles away!) The people of Shechem don't like us. They may have harmed your brothers. I want you to try to find them. I must know how they are."

Show Illustration #5

Jacob continued, "The trip won't be easy. The road is rough. Bandits are always hiding, waiting to rob and kill travelers. It will take a long time to go to Shechem. You'll get tired, Joseph. You'll be alone at night. You must take extra care because of the wild beasts which could attack you. But I love your brothers and need to know about them. If they are in trouble, we must help them."

Because of father-love, Jacob sent Joseph. He would miss Joseph. He knew the journey would be dangerous. Yet Jacob was willing to risk the life of his beloved son for the sake of the sons who were far away.

2. JOSEPH OBEYS HIS FATHER
Genesis 37:13-17

Joseph replied, "Yes, Father, we must help them. I'll go–gladly."

Show Illustration #6

Without hesitation, Joseph obeyed. He left Hebron where he enjoyed the company of his father. Off he went on the long, lonely search for his brothers.

The days were hot. The nights were cold. When he finally reached Shechem, his brothers were nowhere in sight. He pushed on from one pasture to another, searching carefully, but without success.

Observing Joseph's hunt, a man asked, "For whom are you looking?"

"I am looking for my brothers, Reuben, Simeon, Levi, Judah–ten of them altogether," Joseph replied. "Have you seen them? Do you know where they are feeding their flocks?"

"Oh, yes, I remember them. They were here. But as you can see, they've gone." The man continued, "I heard them say they were going to Dothan to find pasture."

Dothan! Ten more miles to hike! Joseph could have turned back. Apparently his brothers had not been harmed by the people of Shechem. He had learned where they had gone. He could've reported this to his father.

But Joseph knew his father wouldn't be satisfied. Joseph knew he would have to find them himself. Besides, he, too, loved his brothers. So he trekked on and on, looking this way and that. Then at last, he found them.

Have you been thinking? Did you see in Joseph's life any shadows or any likenesses to the Lord Jesus? (*Teacher:* Have students share their observations.) What about Jacob's concern for his missing sons? Of whom does Jacob remind us?

3. THE LORD JESUS, SENT BY HIS FATHER
John 3:16; 1 John 4:10

Jacob's love for his sons is like the heavenly Father's love for us. We are far away from God because of sin. God hates sin. It separates all of us from Him. (See Isaiah 59:2.) He created us in His own image and likeness. (See Genesis 1:26.) Alas, we have all fallen short of what God planned for us to be! (See Psalm 14:1-3; Romans 3:10-18, 23.) Instead of being like Him, we choose to sin. (See Isaiah 53:6.) And sin must be punished. But God still loves us. He wants us for Himself.

Show Illustration #7

That is why, before time began, God the Father and God the Son planned what They would do.

Since then they have done exactly as They'd planned. The Father sent His only Son to earth. (See 1 John 4:14.) Leaving all the wonders of Heaven, Christ came as a tiny baby and was laid in a manger bed. Because He is God the Son, He lived a perfect life. When He grew into manhood, God placed on Him all the sins of all people everywhere. (See Isaiah 53:6; 2 Corinthians 5:21; 1 Peter 2:24.) For those sins, Christ gave His own precious blood. (See John 10:17-18; Romans 5:8; 1 Peter 1:19-20; 1 Corinthians 15:3-4.) He took our awful punishment for sin–death. (See Matthew 20:28; Mark 10:45; Romans 6:23; 1 Peter 3:18; 1 John 2:2.) Oh, what it cost the Lord Jesus to pay for our sins! But having paid the price, God raised Him from the dead. (See Matthew 28:5-6; Acts 2:24, 32; 3:15, 26; 4:10; 5:30; 13:28-30; 1 Corinthians 15:3-4.)

God the Father and Christ the Son are far greater than Jacob and Joseph. But here are some likenesses:

Jacob sent the son of his special love to find the missing brothers. In the same way, God sent His beloved Son to find us who are lost in sin.

As Joseph left his father's home, so the Lord Jesus left the glories of His Father's heavenly home.

4. THE LORD JESUS OBEYS HIS FATHER
Luke 19:10; John 4:34; 5:30

Joseph gladly obeyed his father, not minding the cost. The Lord Jesus obeyed His Father. He paid the full price–His own precious blood–to bring to God all those who trust in Him.

Joseph determined to do exactly what his father said. and just like Joseph, the Lord Jesus said, "I seek the will of the Father who sent Me" (John 5:30). (See John 4:34; Hebrews 10:7.)

Why did God send the Lord Jesus to earth? (*Teacher:* Question your students concerning the love of God, our sin and the need for a Saviour.)

The Lord Jesus knew His time on earth would not be easy. He knew He would get hungry, thirsty and tired–as others do. He knew He would be hated. He knew how dreadful His death for us would be. But none of these things kept Him from obeying His Father. Like His Father, He too loves sinners. And He was willing to seek sinners and save them by His blood. (See Luke 19:10; Philippians 2:6-8.)

Show Illustration #8

Now the Lord Jesus is again with God the Father in beautiful Heaven. And they want you to be with them someday. Do you believe that Jesus is the Son of God? Will you place all your trust in Him? Will you ask Him to forgive your sins? If so–and if you truly mean it–He will accept you into His family now. And, in His time, you'll be with Him in Heaven. (See John

10:28.) There, forever and forever, you'll remember that by His precious blood Jesus made it possible. (See Revelation 5:9-12.)

If you are already a child of God, can you honestly say, as the Lord Jesus did, "I always do those things which please my Father"? (See John 8:29.) Are you His obedient child? He says, "Love one another" (John 15:17). Have you obeyed this command? Is there someone–another Christian, perhaps–whom you haven't loved as you ought? List some things you could do this week to show love for him or her.

God commands: "Do not worry, saying, 'What will I eat?' or 'What will I drink?' or 'What will I wear?' But take care of the things of God first. Be right with Him. Then He will take care of these other things" (Matthew 6:25, 31-33). Are you worrying? Or are you obeying God by trusting Him?

Does someone have something against you? God commands that even before giving a gift to Him, you should go to that person. Set matters straight so you can agree with each other again. *Then* give to God. (See Matthew 5:23-25.) Have you obeyed this command? List in your notebook anyone who may be against you. Decide now when you'll see them to ask their forgiveness. Write this in your notebook.

Have you forgiven anyone who may have wronged you? God commands you to do this. (See Matthew 18:21-35.) Could you count how many times you have sinned against God? Probably not. Yet He has forgiven you. Since He has forgiven you so much, the least you can do is to forgive others. (See Ephesians 4:32.) Will you obey His command? List the names of any who have wronged you. Determine now when you will offer them forgiveness. Enter this in your notebook.

Now let's ask our heavenly Father to make us as truly obedient as the Lord Jesus.

Lesson 3
RELATIONSHIP WITH BROTHERS (Part 1)

NOTE TO THE TEACHER

Old Testament study is interesting. There is much to be learned from the normal, everyday lives of those who were on earth at that time. Certain people, however, had extraordinary experiences planned by God Himself. Their circumstances were similar to others which would occur hundreds of years later in New Testament times.

Bible study grows from interesting to fascinating when we find New Testament truths in the Old Testament. On occasion God points out particular similarities. (See, for example, Matthew 12:40; John 3:14; 1 Corinthians 10:4.) These Old Testament facts are known as "types." They are examples of New Testament accounts. They teach us spiritual lessons. Once, when a few Old Testament incidents are mentioned, we are told, ". . . These were our examples [they happened as types for us], to the intent we should not lust after evil things, as they also lusted . . . These things happened unto them for ensamples [as types]: and they are written for our admonition . . ." (1 Corinthians 10:6, 11).

The careful student will observe that Joseph isn't named in the New Testament as a type of Christ. Nevertheless, a number of his experiences are similar to those of the Lord Jesus. Joseph's life illustrates beforehand something of Christ's life. These word-pictures are meant to affect our daily living–teachers and students alike!

Scripture to be studied: Genesis 37; verses mentioned in the lesson.

The *aim* of the lesson: The Old Testament account of Joseph and his brothers helps us understand what the Lord Jesus endured for us.

What your students should *know*: The hatred shown toward Joseph by his brothers pictures for us the hatred of the Jews toward another Jew, the Lord Jesus Christ.

What your students should *feel*: Gratitude to Jesus Christ for enduring the hatred of wicked, sinful men.

What your students should *do*:
Unsaved: Receive the Lord Jesus as Saviour from sin.
Saved: Decide how they can show Christ's love to those who treat them hatefully.

Lesson outline (for the teacher's and students' notebooks):
1. Joseph, hated by jealous brothers (Genesis 37:3-4).
2. Joseph, hated because he dreamed of becoming a ruler (Genesis 37:5-11).
3. The Lord Jesus, hated by jealous Jewish leaders (Matthew 27:18; John 5:18; 10:31-33).
4. The Lord Jesus, hated because He said He would be King (Matthew 26:64).

The verse to be memorized:
God was with him, And delivered him out of all his afflictions. (Acts 7:9b-10a)

THE LESSON

Do you know how it feels to be hated–really hated? When you see the person who hates you, how do you feel? What do you do? What do you say? (*Teacher:* Encourage discussion.)

Joseph, who lived in Old Testament times, was hated. That hatred came from one, two, three, six, eight, ten others! And they were all his brothers. Imagine that! Why did they hate him? What did Joseph do about it? These are the subjects of our study today.

We have already seen that Joseph is like the Lord Jesus Christ in four ways:
1. Joseph was Jacob's beloved son. The Lord Jesus is God's beloved Son.
2. Joseph enjoyed being with his father, Jacob. Jesus Christ enjoyed being with His Father, God.
3. Joseph was sent by his father to find his brothers who were far from home. Jesus was sent to the earth by His Father to seek those who are lost.
4. Joseph was obedient to his father. The Lord Jesus was obedient to His Father.

(*Teacher:* It would be good to show the first eight illustrations and ask the students to mention these four similarities. Also refer to inside back cover, reminding them that the two men lived about 1,900 years apart.)

Because Joseph's life was like a shadow of the life of the Lord Jesus, we think of Christ as we study Joseph. How Christ treated those who hated Him are examples for us to follow. Listen carefully!

Joseph's ten older brothers were a heartache to their father, Jacob. They'd grown up while Jacob was working for his uncle Laban. They'd seen their father scheme and trick others to get what he wanted. It never mattered to him that he hurt others. In those days, Jacob didn't care much about God. Nor was he interested in what God wanted for his life. He was a poor example to his sons and didn't teach them properly about God.

They all remembered that morning when their father limped into camp. How changed he was after that! Instead of scheming, Jacob talked about God's will for his life. For the first time, they saw their father build an altar and worship God.

1. JOSEPH, HATED BY JEALOUS BROTHERS
Genesis 37:3-4

The Bible doesn't record the conversations of Joseph's brothers. But out in the fields as they cared for their flocks, they had lots of time to talk. What they said could've been like this:

"What has happened to our father? All he talks about is obeying God and serving Him," Reuben, the oldest, said.

Levi added, "Yes, and he says we did wrong when we killed the men at Shechem who mistreated our sister, Dinah. According to him, we should let God take care of our enemies instead of getting revenge ourselves."

Another brother spoke up, "Joseph is the only one who can please our father. He thinks everything Joseph does is right. The two of them are always talking together about the plan of God for our family."

"And now Reuben's birthright privileges are gone. Even though he is the oldest, our father made that beautiful robe for Joseph. This proves that Joseph is to be the heir." The brothers all agreed.

"I hate Joseph!" one exclaimed.

"I hate him, too!" the brothers chorused.

One insisted, "He may strut around in his elegant coat. But we won't let him rule over us."

Show Illustration #9

Every time they saw their brother Joseph, their hatred grew fiercely. They would not have admitted it, but the ten older brothers hated Joseph because they were jealous. They envied the position which their father had given him. Joseph loved his father and tried to please him. He also loved God and wanted to please Him. Joseph's brothers were sinful. Their conduct was evil. The very purity of Joseph's life made them feel guilty!

God says, "Envy is the rottenness of the bones" (Proverbs 14:30). It causes "confusion and every evil work" (James 3:16).

2. JOSEPH, HATED BECAUSE HE DREAMED OF BECOMING A RULER
Genesis 37:5-11

One evening when his brothers came home from the fields, Joseph gathered them together.

Show Illustration #10

"Listen!" he said. "I had a dream last night. We were all working in the fields cutting grain and tying it into bundles. Suddenly my bundle stood straight up and all your bundles bowed down to mine!"

"Do you think you're going to be our king?" his brothers shouted. "Do you think we're going to bow down to you? Well, you'll find out differently!" In their hearts, they hated Joseph more than ever!

Sometime later when the family was together, Joseph announced, "I had another dream. This time the sun and moon and 11 stars bowed down to me."

"Joseph, my son!" Jacob began rebukingly. "Do you mean that your mother and I, as well as your brothers, are going to bow down to you?"

To himself Jacob thought, *I wonder what these dreams mean. Is God revealing His future plans to Joseph? Maybe he really will be a ruler someday.* Jacob said no more about it.

Now Joseph's brothers were completely turned against him. "So he thinks both we and our parents will bow to him! Absurd! That young dreamer needs to be put in his place. We'll never bow to him! He'll never be our ruler!" And their hatred grew more. Were they afraid there might be some truth in Joseph's dreams?

3. THE LORD JESUS, HATED BY JEALOUS JEWISH LEADERS
Matthew 27:18; John 5:18; 10:31-33

Just as Joseph's brothers hated him, so God's ancient people, the Jews, hated Christ. They hated Him, even though Christ was born into a Jewish family. The Jewish leaders hated Jesus because they were *jealous* of Him. (See Matthew 27:18.)

Many people followed Jesus because He healed and fed them. Some followed because He taught them about God the Father. He taught them about sin and how sins could be forgiven. He taught about Heaven and how they could go there. This made the Jewish leaders so angry they wanted to kill Jesus.

They hated Jesus because of who He said He was. "He says God is His Father. He claims to be equal with God. He is a blasphemer and a liar! Jesus is only a man. He should be stoned!" the Jews shouted (John 5:18; 10:31-33; 15:23-25). "What right does He have to say He came down from Heaven? He came from Nazareth!" (See John 6:41-42.)

Show Illustration #11

When Jesus was in His hometown, Nazareth, He told them He was the promised One sent by God. This made them furiously angry. The men shouted: "We've got to get rid of Him!" *But how?* they wondered. Then they had an idea. "Let's take Him to the top of the hill and shove Him off!" (*Teacher:* Hide illustration #11.)

That was exactly what they tried to do. They mobbed Jesus, forced Him outside the city and to the hilltop. But the Lord Jesus simply (miraculously!) walked through the crowd and went on His way!

Jesus Christ came to His own people, the Jews. But most of them refused to accept Him as God's Son. (See John 1:11.) They hated Him because their deeds were evil. Jesus told them, "You dress up in beautiful robes and look clean on the outside. But your hearts are full of sin." (See Matthew 23:27.) He said that God the Father loved Him. (See John 5:20; 15:9.) So, because of the Father's love, the Jews hated the Lord Jesus.

4. THE LORD JESUS, HATED BECAUSE HE SAID HE WOULD BE KING
Matthew 26:64

Joseph's brothers hated him when he told them his dreams. They refused to believe that they would bow down to him, as the dreams had revealed. And when the Lord Jesus told the Jews that He would be their King, they hated Him.

They should not have been surprised. Even before He came to earth, the angel Gabriel had told Mary that, by a miracle, she would be the mother of God's Son. And, the angel said, "He will rule over the house of Jacob [the Jews] forever. His kingdom will never end." (See Luke 1:31, 33.) Many must have heard that word.

Later some wise men asked, "Where is the newly born King of the Jews? We saw His star back East in our country. We have come to worship Him." (See Matthew 2:2.) When they asked for another King, Herod became furious, because he was the king over the Jews at that time. He went into such a rage that everyone must have learned that the King of the Jews was on earth. (See Matthew 2:13-16.)

Many years later, when the Lord Jesus rode into Jerusalem on a donkey, crowds of people ran before Him. They praised God saying, "Blessed is the King who comes in the name of the Lord." (See Luke 19:38.)

This made the Jewish leaders so angry that they commanded Jesus to make the people be quiet. But Jesus answered, "If I would silence them, the stones would immediately cry out" (Luke 19:39-40).

The Jewish leaders were even more determined to do away with Christ. Every time He claimed to be their King, they hated Him more. "All the people are following Him," the Jews agreed angrily. "We have to get rid of Him."

That week they arrested Jesus. On trial, He said, "One day you'll see Me sitting at the right hand of the all-powerful God. You'll see Me coming in the clouds." (See Matthew 26:64.)

Show Illustration #12

This made the Jewish leaders furious. They spit in Jesus' face. They slapped Him. They shouted, "He is guilty! Put Him to death!" (See Matthew 26:65-68.)

Why did God the Son endure the awful treatment of wicked men? He could've destroyed them all instantly. He could've returned to Heaven immediately. Instead, He humbled Himself. He suffered their abuse. Why? Because He loved them. And He loves us. He loves you. He, the perfect One, suffered and died for your sins. Do you believe He is the Son of God? Will you admit you are a sinner? Will you place all your trust in Him and ask Him to forgive your sin? If you do, He will receive you as His child. Will you trust Him right now?

Both Joseph and the Lord Jesus knew the pain of being hated. But neither fought back. Why? Because they loved those who hated them. God commands us who belong to Christ to follow His example. He did not sin. No lies or bad talk came from His lips. Although people spoke against Him, He didn't speak back. He suffered from what people did to Him. But He didn't try to pay them back. Jesus put Himself in God's hands knowing that God always does right. (See 1 Peter 2:21-23.)

Does someone hate you because you have trusted in Christ Jesus? Will you determine, with God's help, to do as Jesus did toward those who hated Him?

Lesson 4
RELATIONSHIP WITH BROTHERS (Part 2)

Scripture to be studied: Genesis 37; Mark 12:1-12; all verses cited in the text.

The *aim* of the lesson: God allows tests (even the hatred and jealousy of others) to strengthen our Christian character.

What your students should *know*: Tests which come to them now will help make them more useful to God.

What your students should *feel*: Gratitude that though people may be against them, God is always for His own.

What your students should *do*: Pray for and seek ways of helping those who hate them because they belong to Christ.

Lesson outline (for the teacher's and students' notebooks):

1. Joseph schemed against by his brothers (Genesis 37:12-25).
2. Joseph, sold by his brothers (Genesis 37:25-35).
3. The Lord Jesus, schemed against by Jewish leaders (Mark 12:1-12; 14:1-2).
4. The Lord Jesus, sold by a disciple (Mark 14:10-11, 43-46).

The verse to be memorized:

God was with him, And delivered him out of all his afflictions. (Acts 7:9b-10a)

NOTE TO THE TEACHER

With this lesson, we are halfway through our study of the similarities between Joseph and the Lord Jesus. The life of each helps to explain and enlarge upon the other. So it is throughout the Word of God. There are many likenesses between certain Old and New Testament people, things and events. Look for them as you study. Remember, however, that having lots of knowledge about the Bible is not enough. It *must* affect your life and works for good. It is your responsibility, teacher, to grow as a Christian. (See 2 Timothy 3:16-17; 2 Peter 3:18.)

Refer again, please, to the inside back cover. Remind your students that Joseph lived about 1,900 years before the Lord Jesus.

REVIEW

Before beginning the lesson, review the first six likenesses between Joseph and the Lord Jesus Christ.

1. Joseph was Jacob's beloved son. The Lord Jesus is God's beloved Son. (Show Illustration #3.)

2. Joseph enjoyed being with his father. The Lord Jesus enjoyed fellowship with His Father. (Show Illustration #4.)
3. Joseph was sent by his father to find his brothers. The Lord Jesus was sent to earth by His Father to seek the lost. (Show Illustration #7.)
4. Joseph was obedient to his father. The Lord Jesus obeyed His Father in coming to seek sinners. (Show Illustration #8.)
5. Joseph was hated because his brothers were jealous of him. The Lord Jesus was hated because the Jewish leaders were jealous of Him. (Show Illustration #11.)
6. Joseph was hated because he dreamed of becoming a ruler. The Lord Jesus was hated because He said He would be King. (Show Illustration #12.)

THE LESSON

Did you ever make a special gift for someone you loved? It was for a particular occasion–birthday or Christmas, perhaps. You wanted with all your heart to surprise the receiver. Yet you were so pleased you gave many broad hints, practically telling beforehand what the gift was. (*Teacher:* Your students may want to tell such experiences which they have had.)

Even before the world was created, God the Father and God the Son planned a wonderful gift for all people everywhere. Together they would make it possible for everyone to have forgiveness of sin. All who have sins forgiven would be with them forever in Heaven. What a gift! From the very beginning, God gave hints about His gift. (See Genesis 3:15.) From time to time He caused certain people to have experiences like those His Son would have on earth. It was as if He whispered, "My gift to you will be like this." Joseph, whom we have been studying, is a good picture of God's gift of love.

1. JOSEPH SCHEMED AGAINST BY HIS BROTHERS
Genesis 37:12-25

Joseph's brothers were tending their flocks in Dothan. They were surprised when they saw someone climbing the hillside.

"Who is that?" one asked.

Squinting and shading his eyes, a brother exclaimed, "It's Joseph, the dreamer! What does he want?"

Another suggested, "Now is our chance to get rid of him. Let's kill him!"

"A great idea! We can throw his dead body in a hole. No one will ever know what happened to him."

"What will we tell our father when we get home and he asks about Joseph?" several wanted to know.

"We could say some wild beast killed him."

"That will serve him right. He thinks he's going to be our ruler. We'll see what'll become of his wonderful dreams!"

Reuben, the oldest, objected. "Listen, brothers! Let's not kill Joseph. There's an empty well over there. Just throw him in it. It is so deep he'll never be able to get out. He'll simply die down there. That way we can get rid of him without shedding blood."

Walking away, Reuben thought to himself, *When they leave, I'll pull Joseph out of the well. Then he can go home to our father. I won't tell my brothers.* And off he went by himself.

When Joseph got closer he greeted his brothers happily. "I'm glad I found you. Father's been concerned about you. Are you all right? Where's Reuben?"

Instead of welcoming Joseph, they grabbed him roughly. "Let me go!" he shouted. "What are you doing? Be careful! You will tear my coat!"

His brothers shrieked: "That is exactly what we want to do!" . . . "We *are* destroying your beautiful coat!" . . . "Do you think you're going to rule over us?" . . . "What makes you think you'll be our father's heir?"

They tore off his coat and threw him into the empty well.

"See how your dreams turn out down there!" they snorted.

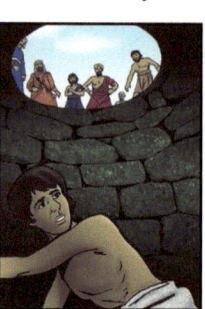

Show Illustration #13

"Judah! Dan! Levi! Don't leave me down here!" Joseph begged. "Please get me out. PLEASE! I came to see if you're all right. I came with greetings from our father. He loves you. He was afraid some harm had come to you. Please get me out of here!"

But Joseph's brothers ignored him. They acted as if they were deaf. (See Genesis 42:21.)

One said, "I'm hungry."

"I am, too!" the others agreed. So the nine sat down and ate their lunch as if nothing had happened.

Jealousy and hatred had made them hard. They had no love, no mercy, for their brother. He had done nothing to them. He loved them. He had come this long, dangerous journey to find out about *them*.

2. JOSEPH SOLD BY HIS BROTHERS
Genesis 37:25-35

"Which of us will our father choose for his heir now?" Joseph's brothers wondered as they sat eating.

They laughed when they heard Joseph pleading from the well, "Help me! Please get me out of this pit. What will Father say if you let me die here? PLEASE HELP ME!"

But his brothers paid no attention. "Look!" Judah exclaimed. "There's a caravan of camels. They're loaded with spices and herbs! They are going to Egypt. We can sell Joseph to them. He'll make a good slave. Since he's our brother, we might feel guilty if we killed him. Come on! Let's sell him!"

"That's a great idea!" they all agreed.

Yanking Joseph out of the pit, they hurried him down to the traveling merchants.

They called, "We have a slave here! Would you like to buy him? How much will you pay? He is young and strong and worth a lot!"

Show Illustration #14

Looking him over, the merchants bargained back and forth with Joseph's brothers. Finally they agreed to pay 20 silver pieces for him.

His brothers returned to their flocks jingling the silver.

"Good riddance!" they laughed. "Now we won't have to listen to Joseph's dreams about himself!"

Later, when Reuben returned, he saw the pit was empty. He ran to his brothers, demanding, "What have you done with Joseph?"

"We sold him! Look at this!" And they dangled the silver before Reuben.

"You sold him?" Reuben wailed. "Oh, what will I do? This will break our father's heart. What can we tell him?"

"Do not be upset, Reuben. Let's kill a lamb and dip Joseph's coat in the blood. When our father sees it, he'll think a wild beast killed Joseph. And we won't have to say a thing!"

Later, when Jacob saw the coat, he was brokenhearted. No one could comfort him. Believing Joseph to be dead, he told his family, "I will mourn for him the rest of my life."

Joseph's brothers went about their work as usual. They tried, but they couldn't wipe from their memories the sound of Joseph's pitiful pleading. Their consciences troubled them constantly and a feeling of guilt haunted them (Genesis 42:21).

Poor Joseph! Hated, schemed against, sold by his brothers.

3. THE LORD JESUS, SCHEMED AGAINST BY JEWISH LEADERS
Mark 12:1-12; 14:1-2

Hundreds of years later the Lord Jesus also was hated. Leaving the glories of Heaven, He came to earth to seek all who were separated from God by sin. He went about doing good. But many–even the religious leaders–hated Him. Why? They were jealous of Him. Instead of receiving Him as their Saviour from sin, they planned how they might get rid of Him.

Christ Jesus knew how they felt. To let them know that He understood what they were thinking, He told them a story. (See Mark 12:1-12.)

He said that a man planted a vineyard (a garden of grapes). He hired some farmers to care for it after which he moved to another country. When it was time to pick the ripe grapes, he sent one of his servants to collect his share of them. But the farmers beat the servant and sent him back empty-handed.

The owner sent a second servant. They treated him even worse. And he returned with severe head injuries. When the third servant came, the farmers killed him.

After many servants were either injured or killed, the owner called his beloved only son. "I want you to go to my vineyard," the farmer said. "Bring the grapes to me. The farmers have mistreated my servants. But you, my son, they will respect."

The son obediently went on his father's errand. Seeing him, the farmers said to each other, "Look! The owner's son is coming! He'll own this vineyard when his father dies. Let's kill him. Then the vineyard will be ours!" And immediately they murdered him.

When the owner heard what had happened, he came and killed the farmers, then rented his vineyard to others.

Show Illustration #15

The Jewish leaders, when Jesus told them this story, knew He was talking about them. They understood He was saying that they refused to respect Him, God's beloved Son. For this, they themselves would be destroyed. They wanted to grab Him and get rid of Him right then.

4. THE LORD JESUS, SOLD BY A DISCIPLE
Mark 14:10-11, 43-46

Again and again the Jewish leaders wanted to kill Jesus. But they were afraid of the people, many of whom believed He was truly the promised One sent by God.

Finally, Judas, one of Jesus' disciples, went to the leaders, "I know you would like to arrest my Master," he said. "How much will you pay me if I take you to Him?" (See Matthew 26:15.)

Show Illustration #16

"Thirty silver pieces."

"Fine! Come with me to the garden of Gethsemane. He is praying there right now. I'll walk up to Him and kiss Him. This way your soldiers will know, even in the darkness, which One He is." (See Mark 14:43-46.)

Judas had heard Jesus teaching day after day. They had been together for three years. He knew that Jesus claimed to be the Son of God. He had watched Jesus heal the sick and feed the multitudes. How could Judas have done such a thing? He was controlled by another–Satan. And Satan gave him the idea of betraying Jesus and selling him for 30 silver pieces.

Judas had thought it would be nice to have the extra money. But as soon as he finished his wicked deed, he felt so guilty he tried to return the money to the Jewish leaders. When they refused it, Judas threw the money down. And he went out and hanged himself. (See Matthew 27:4-5.)

Both Joseph and Jesus knew the pain of being hated and betrayed by those closest to them. But God was watching from above. He even allowed these things to happen! (See Hebrews 5:8; compare Job 1:8-12; 23:10.)

And God knows all about you. He may be permitting tests (as He did with Joseph) to prepare you for some great work. If you accept the daily problems as from God Himself, He will deliver you. He (the faithful One) will take you through them and can even make you a glowing Christian. (See 1 Corinthians 10:13.)

Please list in your notebook the names of those who may be jealous of you or hate you because you are a Christian believer. We'll pray for them by name and ask God to help you show His love to them today–this week.